AMERICA DEBATES

AMERICA DEBATES STEM CELL RESEARCH

Jeri Freedman

rosen publishing's
rosen
central®

New York

To my niece and nephew, Laura and Matthew Freedman, with love

Published in 2008 by The Rosen Publishing Group, Inc.
29 East 21st Street, New York, NY 10010

First Edition

Library of Congress Cataloging-in-Publication Data

Freedman, Jeri.
America debates stem cell research / Jeri Freedman.
    p. cm.—(America debates)
ISBN-13: 978-1-4042-1928-1
ISBN-10: 1-4042-1928-5
1. Embryonic stem cells—Research—Moral and ethical aspects—Juvenile literature. I. Title.
QH588.S83F74 2007
616'.02774—dc22

                                                2007001036

Manufactured in the United States of America

On the cover: *(Left)* Demonstrators protest President George W. Bush's decision to allow federal funding for stem cell research. *(Right)* A lab technician works with embryonic stem cell cultures.

CONTENTS

Introduction

Stem cells are the basic building blocks from which the cells of every tissue in the body grow. Because of their unique ability to develop into different types of tissue, they could potentially be used to replace tissue damaged or destroyed by disease.

There are many diseases today for which medical science has no cure. Research into stem cells may offer an answer, but this research is still in its early phase. However, if we can learn how stem cells change into different types of tissue, how to safely implant them into the human body with minimal side effects, and how to successfully apply them to specific diseases, they could revolutionize medicine.

Implementing this research requires a source of stem cells. Adult stem cells can be extracted from tissues such as bone marrow. However, adult stem cells develop into a limited number of types of tissue. Therefore, most researchers believe that the future of stem cell research depends on the use of embryonic stem cells, which come from destroyed human embryos. Other useful stem cells can be obtained from the blood left over in the umbilical cord when a baby is delivered. But the supply of such blood is limited. Therefore, most lines (or generations) of embryonic stem cells are developed from cells taken from the tissue of embryos. It is this use of embryos as a source of stem cells that has generated the bulk of the controversy surrounding stem cell research. In this book, we will look at the various types of ethical issues—questions about what is good and what is bad—that stem cell research poses. We'll look at current issues as well as issues that are likely to arise in the future as treatments are developed, in the United States and worldwide.

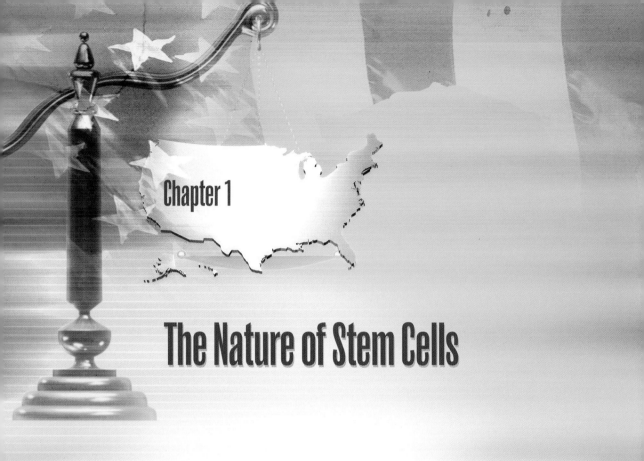

Chapter 1

The Nature of Stem Cells

I n order to understand the controversies surrounding
stem cell research, it is necessary to understand
exactly what stem cells are and what they are used for.

WHAT IS A STEM CELL?

A stem cell gets its name from the fact that it is a basic
type of cell from which many other types of cells develop.
Because stem cells can develop into a wide range of cells,
they could potentially be used to grow new cells to
replace those destroyed by age or disease or by the side
effects of treatment for diseases such as cancer.

There are two categories of stem cells: embryonic stem cells and adult stem cells.

EMBRYONIC STEM CELLS

When the egg and sperm combine, they form a single cell, which divides into two cells, each of which divides to form a cluster of four cells, and so on, until a hollow ball of about 150 cells is formed. This ball of cells is called a blastocyst. It forms four to five days after fertilization. The cells in the inner layer of the blastocyst are embryonic stem cells. The cells in the blastocyst divide repeatedly to form an embryo. As the embryo

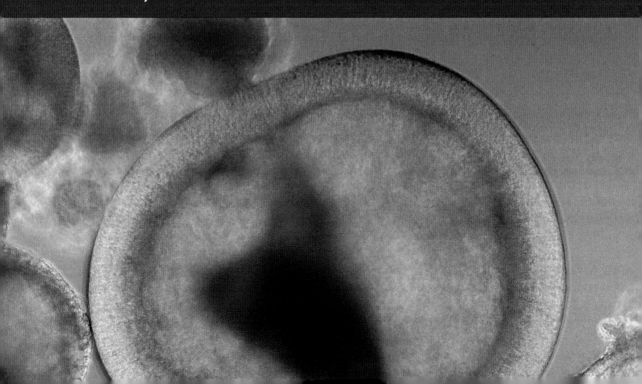

This embryonic stem cell was grown in a research laboratory at Israel's Technion Institute of Technology. The cell has the ability to become any kind of human cell.

grows and develops, the stem cells differentiate, or change, and each takes on the characteristics of a specific type of cell. In cell differentiation, the presence of chemicals in a given bodily environment triggers changes in the cell. Certain genes are switched on in the cell and others are switched off. This leads to the cell developing characteristics, such as size, shape, and ability to secrete a specific compound. In this way, a stem cell becomes a nerve cell, a muscle cell, and so on. Once a stem cell has differentiated into a specific type of tissue cell, it cannot change back.

Stem cells in early embryos have the ability to change into cells found in 200 different types of tissue. Because they can change into all kinds of tissue, they are called totipotent cells. Fully mature cells do not have this level of ability to change. Once a nerve cell or muscle cell is fully developed, it cannot change into another type of cell. Stem cells are able to divide and produce more stem cells for a significant period of time before they change into a specific type of cell. This ability means that scientists can take stem cells from an embryo and produce more stem cells from them. The generations of stem cells produced from a given source of stem cells are called a stem cell line.

ADULT STEM CELLS

The second category of stem cells is adult stem cells. Adult stem cells are immature cells that divide and then replace damaged or dying cells in body tissues. This type of stem cell also is called a somatic stem cell (*somatic* comes from the Greek word

This image of an adult stem cell was taken with a scanning electron microscope. This type of cell is produced in the marrow of the arm and leg bones.

for "body"). These cells are produced primarily in the bone marrow located in the arm and leg bones, and they change into blood and immune system cells. Some are produced by other tissues, but they are present in very small quantities and often do not differentiate into other tissues. Adult stem cells cannot change into as many types of tissue as embryonic stem cells. Some adult stem cells can change into several types of tissue (such as fat, cartilage, bone, or red blood cells and white blood cells); these cells are called multipotent. Others can only produce cells of one type, such as liver cells. These stem cells are called unipotent.

Umbilical Cord Blood Stem Cells

A subset of adult stem cells is umbilical cord blood stem cells. While in the womb, a fetus receives nutrients via its mother's blood through the umbilical cord. When a baby is born, this

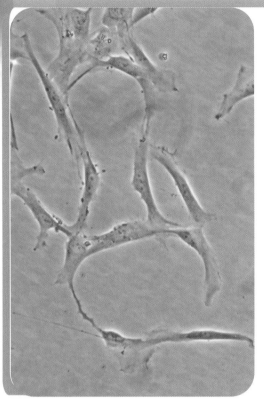

This image shows a type of undifferentiated stem cell. It was taken from umbilical cord blood.

cord is cut. The blood that remains in the cord after it is removed from the baby also contains stem cells. These stem cells are less mature than adult stem cells but more mature than those taken from embryos only a few days old. Scientists can grow these cells in the laboratory, but they will not grow for as long a period of time as early-stage embryonic stem cells.

HOW ARE EMBRYONIC STEM CELLS OBTAINED?

Embryonic stem cells can come from one of three sources:

1. Blastocysts created by fusing egg and sperm cells in vitro (out of the body) in the laboratory.
2. Embryos from terminated pregnancies.
3. Embryos left over from fertility treatments at in vitro fertility (IVF) clinics that otherwise would be discarded.

PIONEERS IN STEM CELL RESEARCH

The field of stem cell research can be traced back to two Canadian researchers: Ernest McCullough and James Till. McCullough is a doctor and Till is a biophysicist (a researcher who studies the physics-based processes in biological organisms). McCullough and Till both joined the Ontario Cancer Institute at Princess Margaret Hospital in 1957 and began to do research work together. In the early 1960s, they performed a series of experiments in which they killed the bone marrow cells in mice by irradiating them and injected normal bone marrow cells into the mice. Lumps appeared in the mice's spleens (the spleen is an organ where blood cells are produced). McCullough and Till believed that the lumps were colonies of cells and that each had grown from a single "stem" cell. Along with graduate student Andy Becker, they subsequently demonstrated that their theory was true, and in 1963, they published a paper in the journal *Nature*. That same year, working with molecular biologist Lou Siminovitch, they were able to demonstrate that the stem cells were self-renewing, further supporting their concept of stem cells. In 2005, McCullough and Till were awarded the Albert Lasker Award for Basic Medical Research.

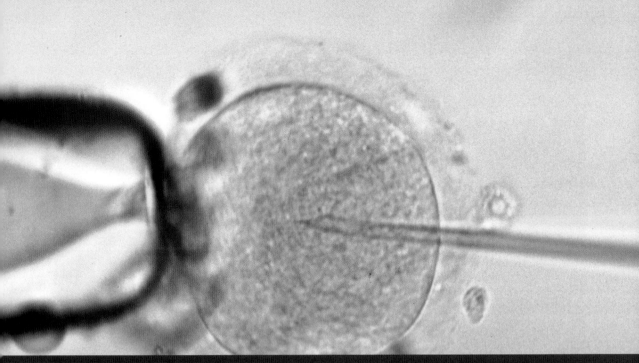

A single sperm is injected into an egg cell during in vitro fertilization. The procedure is usually performed in a glass dish. (*In vitro* means "in glass.")

WHAT RESEARCH IS PRESENTLY BEING PERFORMED?

Some current research is aimed simply at learning what tissues can be produced from stem cells and how best to reproduce and use such cells. Much of this type of research is done in vitro in laboratories. Learning how stem cells change into specific types of cells could result in the ability to stimulate stem cells in laboratories to form specific types of tissue. It could also lead to an understanding of how to stimulate the stem cells present in a patient's body to change into a needed type of cell. The ability to control the process of cell differentiation is very important. Scientists must be able to ensure that all the stem cells fully change into the desired type of tissue in order to avoid negative side effects, such as the formation of tumors (lumps of fast-growing cells), when the cells are implanted in a patient.

Other research consists of using stem cells to experimentally treat diseases that currently can't be cured. Some of this work is carried on by implanting the stem cells in animal models such as mice. However, some experimental medical treatments have progressed to the point where cells are applied to human volunteers. We will explore such experimental treatments in later chapters.

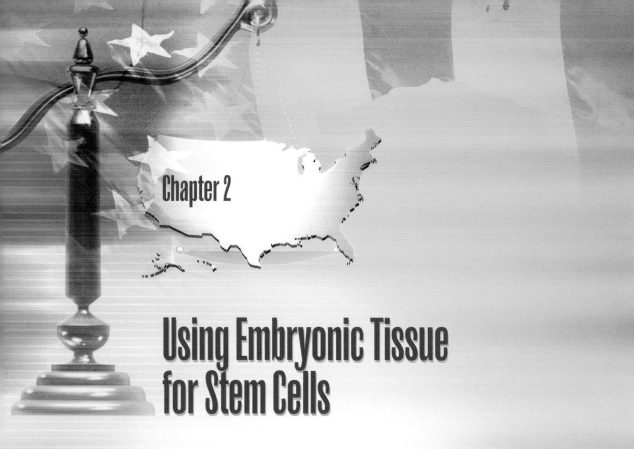

Chapter 2

Using Embryonic Tissue for Stem Cells

Recent research indicates that adult stem cells may be capable of maturing into more types of cells than researchers originally thought. However, it has not been possible to obtain adult stem cells for many types of tissue, such as heart tissue or the special cells of the pancreas that produce the hormone insulin. Insulin is key to treating the disease diabetes, which causes large amounts of the sugar glucose to build up in the blood, damaging blood vessels. Moreover, adult stem cells are present in such tiny amounts that it is hard to obtain an adequate supply of them. Therefore, many researchers feel that embryonic stem cells are the most promising approach for treating many diseases.

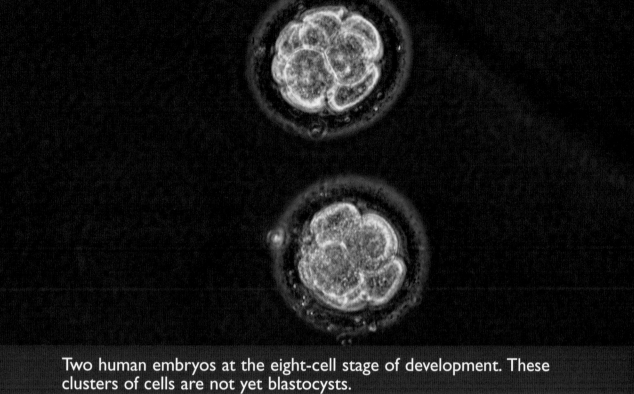

Two human embryos at the eight-cell stage of development. These clusters of cells are not yet blastocysts.

The use of embryonic stem cells has raised many ethical issues, however. As mentioned earlier, there are three major ways to obtain embryonic stem cells: creating blastocysts in the laboratory, extracting the cells from discarded embryos from terminated pregnancies, and from IVF clinics. We will look at the issues surrounding these approaches.

WHAT IS THE STATUS OF AN EMBRYO?

In order to obtain stem cells, scientists first must have an embryo. Regardless of what method they use to generate it, the embryo is still a layer of cells that would eventually develop into the body of a human fetus. This fact brings up a number of ethical questions, including the question of when exactly this change occurs. Is a blastocyst just a layer of cells that will change at some later time into a human fetus? If so, at what point does that change occur?

To a large extent, this is the same question that separates people who are opposed to abortion from those who are in favor of allowing women that option at some point in their pregnancy. Some argue that it is always wrong to create an embryo that isn't going to be implanted in a womb. Others say that to deny potentially lifesaving treatment to ill people is wrong. This ethical issue can be approached from different perspectives.

Time-Based Approach

Some people believe that embryos should have the rights accorded to all people from the moment of conception, or the moment when their genetic material is set. This is the position argued by those who oppose any type of embryonic stem cell research. Others believe that a fetus is not a person until it reaches the state at which it would be able to live outside the womb. In between are those who believe that a blastocyst does not become a fetus until it develops the primitive streak, a structure that will eventually become the spinal cord. Still others believe that a blastocyst acquires the status of fetus once it implants itself in the womb.

Developmental Approach

The developmental approach is more flexible than the time-based perspective. Those who take this approach believe that as the blastocyst develops into a fetus and the fetus develops into a baby, its status changes. As it becomes closer to becoming a "person," it is entitled to greater protections. The difficulty with this approach is establishing exactly when the entity changes from one status to the next.

A second issue with this approach is deciding what criteria should be used to establish "personhood." Is the decisive criterion having a recognizable human form, brain activity, the ability to survive outside the womb, or a particular stage of cognitive development, to name a few characteristics that have been suggested? Those who profess this view do not deny that life is to some degree present from the moment a blastocyst forms, but they hold that the protections due to a blastocyst are not the same as those due to a baby.

WHAT IS AN EMBRYO, ANYWAY?

To confuse matters further, scientists can use chemicals to force an unfertilized egg cell to begin dividing, similarly to an early-stage embryo. However, the resulting mass of cells does not develop beyond the early embryonic stage, and no sperm is combined with the egg. If scientists perform this process, is what they create an embryo or not? Scientists call such artificially created "embryos" parthenotes (from *parthenogenesis*, Greek for "virgin birth") because only an egg cell is used. It is not yet clear whether it will be possible to get useful stem cells from parthenotes, but promising work is ongoing. If it proves possible to extract stem cells from parthenotes, this question will be the source of much debate.

Those who argue that parthenotes are not embryos insist that one must consider why living creatures are given rights and protections. The purpose of such rights is to protect a creature, allowing it to live naturally. They say that a parthenote has no chance to survive or develop into a full-blown embryo and subsequent baby; therefore, rights are of no value to it. Those who argue that parthenotes are still a form of embryo claim that they are alive, and it is not right to kill them.

ETHICS OF USING DISCARDED EMBRYOS

Some people believe that using stem cells from embryos is never acceptable. They believe that it amounts to killing one person to improve the life of another. One question that has arisen is whether it is acceptable to use tissue from embryos left over from fertility treatments. When a couple is trying to conceive children at a fertility clinic, eggs are often removed from the woman and fertilized in a laboratory. Some of the resulting embryos are implanted in her uterus. The embryos that are left over are frozen, in case the treatment is not successful. After some time has elapsed, if the couple does not wish to use the stored embryos, they are destroyed. Some researchers have expressed an interest in using these embryos as a source of embryonic stem cells, since they are going to be destroyed anyway. A similar case can be made for allowing stem cells to be extracted from embryos that are left from legal abortions, because they, too, will be destroyed. Proponents of this approach see it as a matter of doing no harm while increasing the common good. They feel that since aborted fetuses and embryos left over

In 2002, pro-life (anti-abortion) demonstrators in California protested stem cell research outside a conference for pharmaceutical and biotech companies.

from fertility treatments are just going to be thrown out anyway, they would be better used to improve the lives of people who are suffering.

Opposition to Using Discarded Embryos

The Catholic Church and other groups oppose the use of discarded embryos from these sources. They say the fact that the embryos will be destroyed does not justify allowing them to be used for experimentation. According to this position, using discarded embryos is equivalent to killing someone just because that person is going to die anyway. They feel that experimenting on embryos is ethically no different from experimenting on other people. Further, they claim that allowing experimentation

THE RELIGIOUS PERSPECTIVE

Most religious groups have taken a position on embryonic stem cell research. However, what that view is varies not only from religion to religion, but also among different groups within the same religion. Of course, individuals who practice any religion may have a belief that differs from that of the religious authorities. With this in mind, the following are the predominant positions taken by authorities in some of the more prominent religions:

Catholic: According to the United States Conference of Catholic Bishops, the Catholic Church does not oppose stem cell research that uses stem cells derived from adults or umbilical cord blood. It does oppose the harvesting of stem cells from embryonic tissue because the embryo is destroyed in the process. The Catholic Church sees this destruction as the taking of innocent human life.

Hindu/Buddhist: The most common position in traditional Hindu and Buddhist tradition is that personhood begins at conception.

Jewish: It is commonly held in Judaism that embryos less than 40 days old can be used for the purpose of promoting health and sustaining life. Orthodox, Conservative, and Reform (the most conservative to least conservative branches of Judaism, respectively) Jewish authorities all support embryonic stem cell research as long as it is kept within this guideline.

Muslim: Islam does not have a single religious authority. Most clerics believe that embryos gain a soul at 40 to 120 days, depending on the sect in question. Prior to that time, there isn't a religious obstacle to using early-phase embryos.

There are many Protestant sects, and their positions cover the range from the most liberal to the most conservative.

Episcopalian: The Episcopal Church has issued a resolution in support of stem cell research and approved the use of leftover IVF embryos for this purpose, but it does not recommend creating embryos for use.

Lutheran: The Lutheran Church is against the destruction of embryos for the purpose of stem cell research.

Methodist: The United Methodist Church has decreed that the use of leftover IVF embryos for stem cell research is acceptable, but it is against creating embryos for this purpose.

Presbyterian: The Presbyterian Church (USA) has stated its support of stem cell research and recognition that the use of embryos and embryonic tissue may be necessary, within appropriate guidelines.

Southern Baptist: The Southern Baptist Convention has stated firm opposition to the use of embryonic tissue from aborted embryos for research.

Unitarian Universalist: The Unitarian Universalist Church supports the use of leftover IVF embryos for embryonic stem cell research.

An activist demonstrates in front of the Capitol in Washington, D.C. Many concerned about those who suffer from incurable diseases support stem cell research.

on unwanted embryos will lead to acceptance of experimenting on other people who are going to die, such as inmates on death row in prison, terminally ill people, and the like. (This is a form of the "slippery slope" argument discussed in the next chapter, on cloning.)

Although treatments with stem cells show promise, they have also revealed side effects, such as the formation of tumors (lumps)—both benign (noninvasive) and cancerous (likely to spread and invade other organs). In addition, opponents of the use of unwanted embryos claim that there is no proof that successful treatments will result from the destruction of these embryos.

Support for Using Discarded Embryos

Those in favor of allowing stem cells to be derived from embryonic tissue say that their opponents' arguments rest on the idea that allowing such use makes them complicit in the initial "wrongdoing"—the killing of the fetus. They point out that the people who are doing the using are not responsible for the "bad" act and that other people can still benefit. Their position is that the usage of tissue from already deceased embryos is the same thing as transplanting organs from people who die as the result of homicide or suicide. Furthermore, they do not accept the idea that allowing such an experimental use of embryos will inevitably lead to experimentation on fully developed human beings. As a matter of fact, a case could be made that allowing people to die when they might be helped by such research is really no different from manslaughter, or murder due to negligence.

Supporters contend that stem cell experiments in animals already have demonstrated an improvement in many disorders. They hold that treatments will never be successfully developed if experiments are not performed.

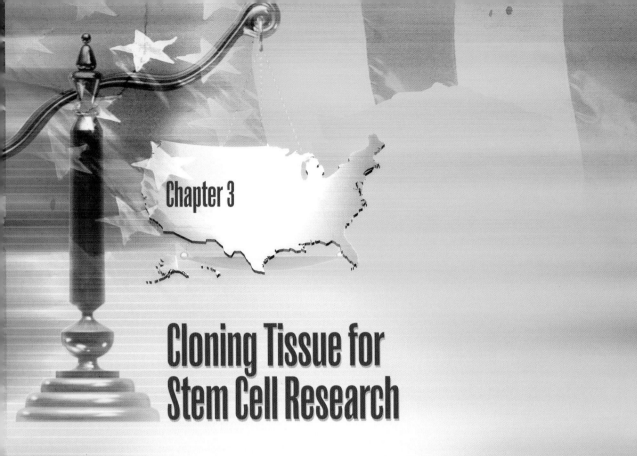

Chapter 3

Cloning Tissue for Stem Cell Research

Cloning is the process of creating an organism that is identical to another organism from which its genetic material is taken. Sometimes cloning is used to create an entire animal. This was the case when Ian Wilmut at the Roslin Institute in Scotland cloned Dolly the sheep in 1996. (See sidebar on page 27.) However, cloning also can be used to simply create more cells that are identical to cells that already exist. This is often done to grow successive generations of the same type of cell in laboratories. The fact that these cells are identical means that their properties are predictable. Using cloned cells, then, scientists can achieve better results in their research.

ETHICS OF CLONING

There are actually two types of cloning: reproductive cloning and therapeutic cloning. When people hear the term "cloning," they usually think of the creation of an entire animal or person, identical to the entity from which the cloned cell was taken. This is reproductive cloning. Therapeutic cloning, on the other hand, is a means of obtaining identical cells for use in laboratory work. The debate about whether to allow therapeutic cloning has been clouded by a lack of understanding of the differences between the two different types.

This photo shows a therapeutic use of human heart stem cells *(blue)*. Researchers used them to repair rat heart tissue *(pink)* damaged by a heart attack.

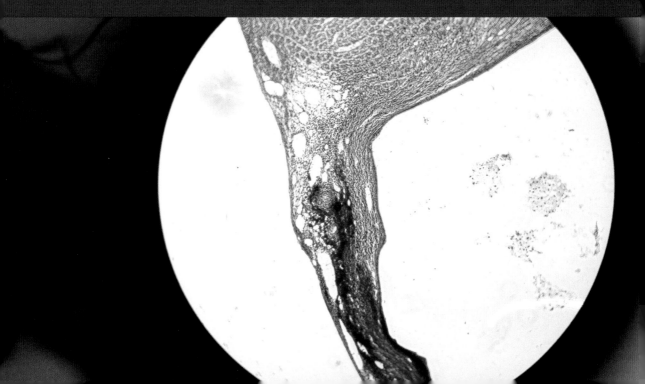

Human Reproductive Cloning vs. Research/Therapeutic Cloning

In human reproductive cloning, a cloned cell would be created with the intent to implant it into a woman's uterus and produce a baby. The baby would, in theory, be an exact biological copy of the person from whom the genetic material was obtained.

In therapeutic cloning, a cell is cloned in order to produce a blastocyst from which stem cells can be obtained. Four to five days after cloning, the inner layer of the blastocyst is removed, and the stem cells in it are cultured in the laboratory to create a cell line. There is no intent to generate an entire fetus from the cloned cells. This fact alone, however, could be either positive or negative, depending on a person's position on the use of embryos in stem cell research. If one believes that an embryo has personhood from the moment of conception, the creation of such blastocysts is unethical and immoral. If one does not hold this belief, then cloning is a safe way of obtaining new stem cell lines without getting into the ethics of using discarded later-stage embryos from abortions or IVF clinics.

Autologous Cloning

Those in favor of allowing the cloning of blastocysts point to an additional important application of cellular cloning—autologous cell cloning. Autologous cloning is the cloning of a patient's own stem cells to produce an adequate tissue-matched supply of such cells to place back in that patient, to treat a disease. The production of autologous stem cells could be a very important application. Using a patient's own genetic material would make

HOW A CLONE IS MADE

First, the nucleus is removed from an egg cell. The nucleus of the cell contains the chromosomes that hold genetic information. Then the nucleus from a cell taken from another source is inserted into the egg. The egg cell is then stimulated so that it divides and grows into an embryo. If the clone is allowed to continue to grow, it will eventually develop into an animal identical to the one from which the genetic material was taken. However, in practice, only a small percentage of the clones that are created actually reach full development. Animals created from cloned cells have exhibited significant health problems, such as shortened life spans and the early onset of diseases usually associated with old age. Therefore, it is unlikely that cloning people will be common practice in the near future.

Dolly, a Finnish Dorset ewe (sheep), created great controversy when she was born in 1996. She was the first mammal successfully cloned using the nucleus from an adult somatic cell.

it less likely that his or her immune system would attack and kill the cells when they are reimplanted. This could greatly increase the chance that a treatment would be a success. However, adult stem cells occur in tiny quantities. Thus, it is difficult to obtain an adequate supply from the patient. Therapeutic cloning would allow genetic material from the patient to be implanted into cells that are allowed to develop into blastocysts that could generate significant quantities of the desired stem cells in the laboratory. The patient could then be treated with his or her own stem cells. Those opposed to any form of cloning can claim that creating an embryo with autologous cells is still creating and killing an embryo. So, once again, the question becomes, To whom is more harm done—the embryo denied life or the patient denied treatment?

THE SLIPPERY SLOPE

Those who oppose all cloning are concerned that allowing any cloning of cells will start us on a downward path that will ultimately lead to an acceptance of cloning in all its forms—including people. This is referred to as a "slippery slope" issue in legal circles. The concern is that if one allows cloning on a limited scale, then little by little that scale will expand to encompass ever more allowable levels. For example, if scientists are allowed to clone a patient's own cells for reimplanting, they'll press for the freedom to clone cells for implantation in relatives, then strangers, then for the ability to clone embryos, then ultimately people. Some people say that it is better not to start on that path at all.

One could question, however, whether the scale of cloning would inevitably expand to include cloning people. The slippery slope concern assumes that the people who regulate stem cell research—be they government or scientific authorities—are incapable of drawing a "line in the sand" at some point. Many contend that it is possible to allow therapeutic cloning of cells but still disallow the cloning of people, for example. One could make the case that this situation is similar to what has happened with abortions. The permitting of abortions in the first few weeks after pregnancy did not stop authorities from forbidding them after the fetus has reached a certain age.

NEGATIVE EFFECTS ON SOCIETY

Aside from religious objections, opponents of any type of cloning have expressed concern that human cloning, even for therapeutic purposes, may have adverse effects on society. Among other things, they claim that it could:

- Demean the women who donate eggs for the cloning, leading to their being treated merely as providers of a useful resource.
- Belittle human reproduction and parenting, creating a culture in which producing children is treated like a technical process, rather than a precious or sacred gift.
- Lead to a "black market" in donated eggs, whereby women in need of money illegally sell their eggs to researchers in need of reproductive material.

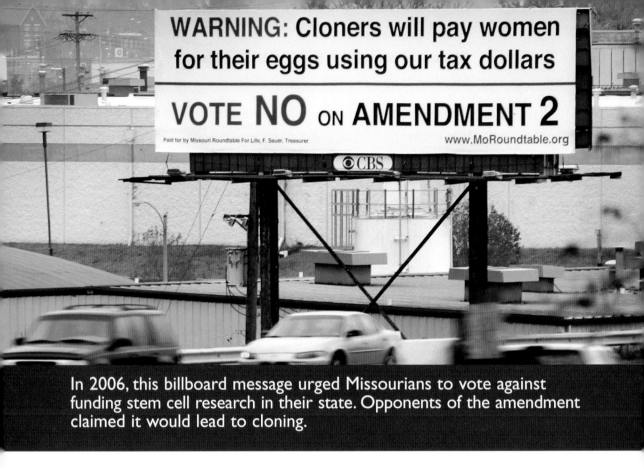

WARNING: Cloners will pay women for their eggs using our tax dollars

VOTE **NO** ON AMENDMENT **2**

Paid for by Missouri Roundtable For Life, F. Sauer, Treasurer

www.MoRoundtable.org

©CBS

In 2006, this billboard message urged Missourians to vote against funding stem cell research in their state. Opponents of the amendment claimed it would lead to cloning.

Those in favor of therapeutic cloning point to the fact that preventing medical treatment that could save lives will have an equally negative effect on society. Society as a whole bears the cost of caring for large numbers of people who suffer from chronic and degenerative diseases. Society loses the contributions of many who, if healthy, could be making a positive impact on the community. Furthermore, denying possible treatment to those who are suffering is inhumane, and thus immoral.

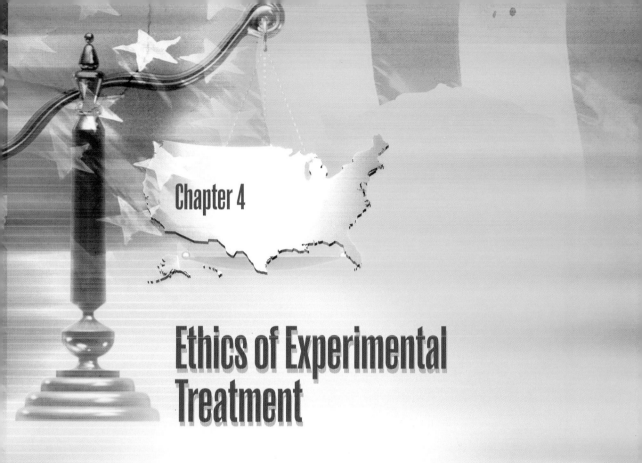

Chapter 4

Ethics of Experimental Treatment

Research is only beginning on the application of stem cells to some diseases. In others, however, research is far enough along to permit the experimental treatment of patients. This chapter explores the issues related to performing experimental medical treatments on human patients.

CURRENT EXPERIMENTAL STEM CELL TREATMENT

Currently, the most widely used application is bone marrow transplantation in patients for whom other forms of treatment have failed. For example, leukemia is a form of blood

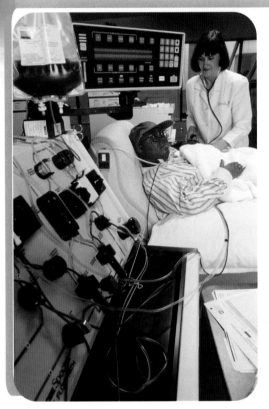

This cancer patient is undergoing stem cell collection before chemotherapy treatment. After treatment, the harvested stem cells can be used to produce new blood cells.

cancer in which white blood cells grow out of control. Doctors have successfully treated some cases of leukemia by killing all the patient's existing bone marrow (the tissue in a person's arm and leg bones that produces stem cells) with radiation or chemotherapy and replacing it with bone marrow from a donor. Ideally, the new bone marrow produces healthy stem cells that grow into cancer-free blood cells. The success of bone marrow transplantation has given researchers hope that it will be possible to transplant stem cells that grow into other types of tissue as well. This would allow doctors to treat many diseases that currently have no cure.

FUTURE TREATMENT ISSUES

So far, most people who have been treated with stem cells have received either adult stem cells or stem cells from umbilical

The future is now: This baby was conceived in vitro specifically so that he would be a good match for donating stem cells to his sister *(center)*, who has a bone marrow disease.

blood. Even though these treatments did not involve the use of embryonic stem cells, such experimental treatments raise a number of ethical issues. Once stem cell research reaches the stage at which the cells can be reliably reproduced and their differentiation controlled, it will be possible to implant the cells in patients. Experiments are already being carried out in some cases using animal models. Early results in animal models for treatment of diseases such as degenerative muscle disease, heart disease, and blindness appear to be promising.

After animal-based research has demonstrated the potential to successfully treat specific diseases, the next step will be the experimental implantation of stem cells in human patients to treat specific diseases. At this point, these implants will be experimental treatments. There will be the potential for unknown interactions with the patient's immune system and the existing tissues into which they are implanted. There will be questions about how the cells will function in their new environment. These are questions that have been encountered with other medical treatments, such as organ transplants, that now are widely accepted. Nonetheless, the use of experimental treatments in human patients comes with its own set of ethical issues.

ARGUMENTS AGAINST ALLOWING EXPERIMENTAL TREATMENT

The following are arguments made by those who oppose testing experimental stem cell treatments in human beings.

Safety

If embryonic stem cells are used for the experimental treatment of disease, this could be dangerous because there are no standards or regulatory procedures in place. For example, there is no way to know whether the embryo from which the stem cells are derived has a disease and/or genetic defect that could be transferred to the patient.

It is not known yet whether such implanted stem cells will grow normally over time. It has been suggested that the implanted stem cells may cause tumors in the patient. Another potential problem is that our immune system attacks foreign tissue. If stem cells are derived from another source (adult or embryo), we might be putting the patient at risk for a severe immune system response that could lead to a greater destruction of tissue, or even death.

Some are concerned that experimental treatments will lead to a preference for testing new medical procedures directly on human beings as a means of establishing their efficacy. They fear that this will lead pharmaceutical manufacturers to test drugs on people before they have been thoroughly tested and their safety is proven.

The stem cells will be implanted among the patient's own cells. These "foreign" cells could potentially be attacked by the patient's immune system cells, causing inflammation and potential damage to existing cells. Immunosuppressive drugs that have been used successfully in organ transplants might offset this problem, but different drugs will have to be tried in order to establish which ones will work. In the meantime, early patients could suffer serious harm.

Informed Consent May Not Really Be Informed

Because of the glory and profit to be gained by successfully developing a cure for a previously incurable disease, researchers could be tempted to downplay the possible negative effects from stem cell implantation. Likewise, they could be tempted to raise unrealistic expectations in patients. Initially, researchers cannot guarantee that just because a cell is of a certain type, it will function successfully in the human body. Will a nerve cell that is supposed to produce the chemical dopamine do so when it has been grown from a stem cell in culture and implanted in the brain ? Will cardiac cells that beat in the laboratory continue to do so when implanted into a patient's damaged heart? If not, it may be possible to address this problem so that the cells can be made to perform correctly. However, the patients who receive cells early in the research may find that the treatment, contrary to their expectations, does not help them.

ARGUMENTS IN FAVOR OF ALLOWING EXPERIMENTAL TREATMENT

The following are arguments made by those who favor allowing experimental stem cell treatments for human patients.

The Patient's Right to Decide

If the patient is adequately informed of the risk, isn't it his or her right to decide whether to take that risk? Over time, performing experimental treatments in people allows procedures to improve and increases the chances of saving other people. A patient who most likely will die from a fatal disease may wish to take advantage of even the slim hope of a cure. Beyond that, the patient may wish to contribute to finding a cure that will spare others his or her fate. This can bring a person peace of mind and improve feelings of self-worth, even if the treatment is not successful.

Condemning the Patient to Death

Do we have the right to deny the chance of survival to the patient, just because that chance is slim or there might be side effects? Are we condemning the patient to death by not permitting him or her to get treatment, even though it is experimental? Is it right to deny a person hope, even though the chance of success might be slight? The issue is even more

Many suffering from degenerative muscle diseases, like this woman testifying before the U.S. Senate, believe that stem cell research holds the key to a cure.

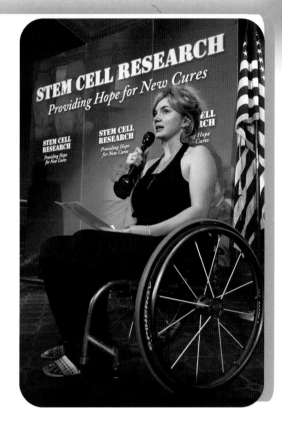

dramatic when the patient is a child. Often, degenerative diseases in children are the result of a genetic defect or inherited disease that will inevitably lead to death. Parents want to give their children every chance to survive, no matter how slight. How can we deny treatment that might save a child who is going to die prematurely?

ACCESS TO STEM CELL TREATMENTS

If stem cell treatments reach the point where they can be used therapeutically to cure diseases, another issue will arise: How can we guarantee equal access to such treatment? This issue will bring with it a whole new set of questions to be answered: How do we guarantee that insurance covers such treatments? How do we provide access to these treatments for those who cannot afford the high cost of health insurance in the United States?

Do industrialized nations with the technology have a duty to provide access to such treatments for those in less developed parts of the world?

Diseases That Could Be Treated with Stem Cells

The following is a list of some of the more common diseases that could someday benefit from stem cell treatments:

Alzheimer's disease (a degenerative brain disease) Replacement of brain cells damaged by the formation of abnormal brain tissue.

autoimmune disorders (diseases in which the body's immune system attacks its own cells) Replacement of abnormal immune system cells with healthy stem cells and/or the replacement of damaged nerve or muscle cells.

blindness Replacement of retinal cells at the back of the eyeball to treat retinal degeneration, which leads to partial or total loss of vision.

brain cancer Replacement of tissue damaged by the disease and by chemotherapy or radiation treatment.

diabetes Replacement of cells in the pancreas that secrete the hormone insulin, which is necessary to digest sugar.

heart disease Replacement of heart cells destroyed by heart disease or heart attacks.

Hodgkin's disease and **non-Hodgkin's lymphoma** (cancers of the immune system) Replacement of defective immune system cells.

inherited genetic disorders Replacement of cells that do not perform properly due to a genetic error. There are many

Former first lady Nancy Reagan supports stem cell research. She believes stem cell treatments may have helped her late husband, President Ronald Reagan, who suffered from Alzheimer's disease.

types of such disorders that affect the ability of a person's body to produce all the necessary chemicals to function.

leukemia Replacement of defective blood cells (currently treated with bone marrow transplants as an experimental stem cell treatment).

lupus (A disease in which immune system cells damage organs and joints).

multiple sclerosis (A disease in which immune system cells attack the insulating layer of cells around nerves, leading to nerve, muscle, and sensory problems).

muscular dystrophy (a disease in which muscle wastes away and is replaced by scar tissue) Replacement of destroyed muscle cells.

ovarian cancer Replacement of tissue damaged by the disease and treatment.

Parkinson's disease Replacement of dead or damaged brain cells that produce the chemical compound dopamine, which is necessary for proper control of muscles by the brain.

renal cell (kidney) cancer Replacement of tissue damaged by the disease and treatment.

rheumatoid arthritis (A disease in which immune system cells attack tissue in the joints).

sickle cell disease Children with this disease produce abnormal red blood cells, leading to disability and death. Implantation of stem cells that will differentiate into healthy red blood cells could address this problem.

small-cell lung cancer Replacement of tissue damaged by the disease and treatment.

spinal cord injury Replacement of nerve cells destroyed by an accident that leaves a person paralyzed.

stroke (bleeding in the brain that destroys brain cells) Replacement of brain cells destroyed by the stroke.

testicular cancer Replacement of tissue damaged by the disease and treatment.

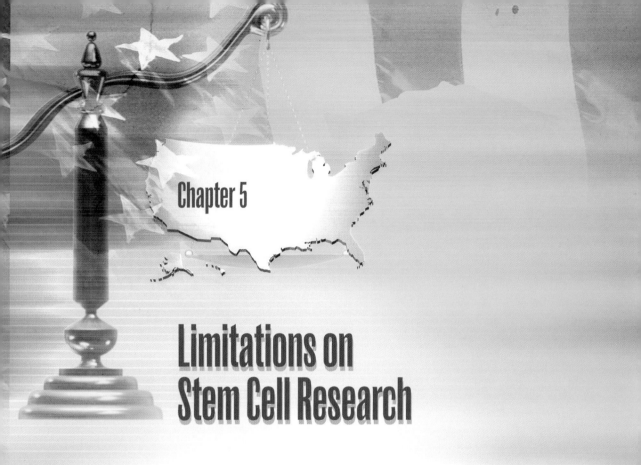

Chapter 5

Limitations on Stem Cell Research

On August 9, 2001, President George W. Bush discussed the issue of stem cell research in a televised speech. He called the issue "one of the most profound of our time," and admitted that there was great disagreement among scientists, ethicists, and other biomedical professionals. In his speech, the president declared that some federally funded research would be allowed using stem cell lines developed prior to that date. However, federal funding would not be provided for research using embryos to obtain new stem cell lines. Individual states, he added, are free to allow stem cell research, as long as it is not funded with federal money. Not surprisingly, President Bush's ruling caused dismay on both sides of the stem cell debate.

ARGUMENTS IN FAVOR OF EXPANDING THE BAN

Those against embryonic stem cell treatment claim that the decision does not go far enough to stop embryonic stem cell research. They see it as justifying the use of stem cells obtained from fetuses on the basis that the fetuses are already dead, so using their cells can't do further harm to them. Moreover, they say that if stem cell research using the existing cell lines succeeds, the demand for stem cells will exceed the current supply. This will require additional sources of stem cells. If the results are not successful, this will create a demand for newer and better cell lines. Either way, allowing stem cell research, even with existing cell lines, is opening the door to trouble.

ARGUMENTS FOR ELIMINATING THE BAN

Those in favor of stem cell research feel that the decision has limited the resources available to do research. Many of the existing cell lines are contaminated and less advanced than new stem cell lines being developed today. They believe that not being able to access new and better sources of embryonic stem cells will interfere with their ability to develop much-needed treatments for debilitating diseases and to access treatments being developed in other countries.

Those who question the validity of withholding funding for embryonic stem cell research point to the fact that other countries are proceeding with such research. For example, according to an article in the *International Herald Tribune*, "EU to

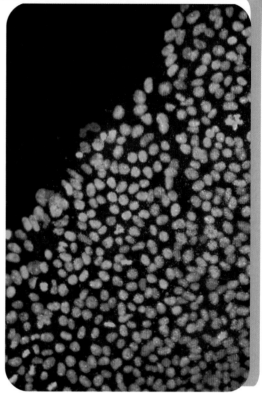

These human embryonic stem cells are contaminated by mouse "feeder cells," which helped them grow. Stem cell lines approved for research by U.S. federal law are similarly contaminated.

Fund Stem Cells," on July 24, 2006, the European Union agreed to provide $64 billion for embryonic stem cell research. This research will use stem cells obtained from embryos that would otherwise be discarded, such as those from fertility clinics. Although individual EU countries are free to ban such research (the case in several predominantly Catholic countries, such as Italy, Poland, and Ireland), the decision clears the way for countries that wish to pursue such research.

An August 17, 2006, article by Wayne Arnold in the *New York Times*, "Singapore Acts as Haven for Stem Cell Research," notes that ES Cell International, a company located in Singapore, has started to offer commercially produced embryonic stem cells for sale over the Internet. The company claims that the stem cells are created in a way that makes them suitable for use in clinical trials. The article states that Singapore's government has shown support for the development of embryonic stem cells through laws and generous financial assistance. The laws in Singapore allow researchers to extract stem cells from embryos slated to be disposed of and from aborted fetuses. They also allow limited cloning of embryos, using cells from those sources. However, embryos produced in this way can be kept for only fourteen days, so there is no significant embryonic development. A November 17, 2006, article on CNN.com, "Iran in the Forefront When It Comes to Stem Cell Research," states that Iran also is actively supporting stem cell research. According to the article, Iran has some of the most liberal laws regarding stem cell research. Since Iranian clerics have agreed that life begins three months after conception, there is no barrier to using early-stage embryos for scientific research.

Dangers of Falling Behind

Those in favor of pursuing embryonic stem cell research in the United States fear that if foreign research leads to medical treatments for currently incurable diseases, American medicine will be left behind. The inability to create new cell lines interferes with federally funded researchers' ability to do top-quality work. In addition, the restriction on using new cell lines makes it impossible for U.S. scientists to work jointly with scientists in other countries that have more liberal laws regarding stem cell research. This means that U.S. scientists are not participating in the newest and most advanced projects, which may produce valuable advances in treating diseases.

This situation can lead to a "brain drain." In other words, talented researchers who would lead advances in such treatments

A California researcher holds vials containing human embryonic stem cells. In 2004, Californians voted to approve $3 billion in state funding for stem cell research.

in the United States are leaving the country to go to Europe or the Far East, where such treatments are being researched. For example, the August 17, 2006, *New York Times* article reported that Neal G. Copeland and Nancy A. Jenkins, two leading American cancer researchers, were leaving the United States to work at the Institute of Molecular and Cell Biology in Singapore.

Although federally funded research is restricted by the ban, state-funded research is not, and some states have taken matters into their own hands. For instance, the British government has formed ties with the California Institute for Regenerative Medicine, which supervises stem cell research in the state of California. The government of the United Kingdom has taken this step because it feels that working with California scientists pursuing research using newer cell lines is likely to be more promising than working with organizations funded by the U.S. government that are restricted to older resources.

Citizens' Welfare

Given the situations just described, one must question whether the current policy of the U.S. government is in the best interests of its own people. In addition, one must ask whether the stem cell research the federal government is funding—research seen as less promising by other countries' governments—is the best use of U.S. taxpayers' dollars. There is little doubt that the United States is falling behind in stem cell research. This is made clear in an October 23, 2006, article on the Center for American Progress Web site, "Minding the Stem Cell Gap," by Jonathan D. Moreno and Sam Berger. The authors state that the number of articles on such research performed by American researchers declined from 33 percent to 25 percent of the total published worldwide from 2002 to 2004.

Finally, the patients could ultimately be leaving, too. If such treatments are developed and/or allowed overseas but not in the United States, those who can afford to will likely go to a foreign country and pay foreign doctors for such treatment.

GENUINE CONCERN vs. POLITICAL SELF-INTEREST

Poll after poll conducted in the past five years has shown that the American public supports embryonic stem cell research. The following are some of the polls conducted in the past year and their results:

- *Newsweek*, October 25–26, 2006: "Do you favor or oppose using federal tax dollars to fund medical research using stem cells obtained from human embryos?" 50 percent in favor, 37 percent opposed, 13 percent undecided.
- *Newsweek*, August 24–25, 2006: "Do you approve or disapprove of the way Bush is handling federal funding for stem cell research?" 31 percent approve, 52 percent disapprove, 17 percent undecided.
- NBC News/*Wall Street Journal*, July 21–24, 2006: "Do you favor or oppose expanding federal funding for embryonic stem cell research . . . ?" 68 percent favor, 27 percent oppose, 5 percent undecided.
- *USA Today*/Gallup Poll, July 21–23, 2006: "As you may know, earlier this week, President Bush vetoed a bill that would have expanded federal funding for embryonic stem cell research. Do you approve or disapprove of his decision to veto this bill?" 37 percent approve, 58 percent disapprove, 6 percent undecided.

There is clearly broad support among Americans for the development of a technology they see as potentially useful. Many believe that stem cell research may lead to treatment for debilitating diseases that they or their loved ones might suffer. This raises the issue of who is being represented by those in the federal government who vote against expanding the range of federally funded stem cell research. On one hand, there are many who have legitimate concerns about embryonic stem cell research. Many of their objections have been discussed in the

OTHER COUNTRIES' POSITIONS ON STEM CELL RESEARCH

How does the U.S. government's position stack up against that of other countries? The following is a list of some countries and their laws regarding embryonic stem cell research.

Australia Allows stem cell research using leftover IVF embryos.

Austria Prohibits all embryonic stem cell research.

Belgium Allows the creation of embryos for research when cell lines from adult or umbilical cord blood are not sufficient.

Canada Allows a range of embryonic stem cell research, with all projects being approved by a national oversight committee.

China Actively supports all stem cell research, including embryonic stem cell projects.

France Allows embryonic stem cell research using leftover IVF embryos.

Germany Prohibits all stem cell research that requires the destruction of embryos.

Iran Actively supports stem cell research.

Ireland Prohibits all embryonic stem cell research.

Israel Allows a wide range of embryonic stem cell research.

Italy Prohibits all embryonic stem cell research.

Japan Allows the creation of embryos for research when cell lines from adult or umbilical cord blood are not sufficient.

Lithuania Prohibits all embryonic stem cell research.

Netherlands Allows embryonic stem cell research using leftover IVF embryos.

Norway Prohibits all embryonic stem cell research.

Poland Prohibits all embryonic stem cell research.

Singapore Actively supports embryonic stem cell research.

South Korea Allows the creation of embryos for research when cell lines from adult or umbilical cord blood are not sufficient.

Spain Allows embryonic stem cell research using leftover IVF embryos.

Sweden Allows the creation of embryos for research when cell lines from adult or umbilical cord blood are not sufficient.

Switzerland Allows the creation of and taking stem cells from embryos.

United Kingdom Allows the creation of embryos for research when cell lines from adult or umbilical cord blood are not sufficient, including the creation and therapeutic cloning of embryos for this purpose.

course of this book. On the other hand, when political leaders are left to decide what research should or should not be allowed, one must ask the question: Are they considering the issue simply on its merits, or are they considering which position is most likely to get them and the members of their political party elected in the next election?

In the case of President George W. Bush and the Republican-controlled Congress that was in power during his first term, the questions raised were: Was the decision to limit federal funding to existing cell lines made with the best interests of

The Missouri Coalition for Lifesaving Cures is one of many organizations pushing for fewer restrictions on stem cell research in the United States.

most Americans in mind? Or was it a decision designed to win them the support of conservative Americans who they believed would vote for them and provide election campaign donations to help them maintain power? Or was the president's decision the reflection of his own personal views? Political considerations such as these are among the reasons that countries such as the United Kingdom, Australia, and Canada have appointed national committees to oversee stem cell research. Would the establishment of an independent committee to regulate stem cell research benefit the United States as well?

IS IT POSSIBLE TO CONDUCT EMBRYONIC STEM CELL RESEARCH ETHICALLY?

Those in favor of embryonic stem cell research point out that this is not the only area of medical treatment in which people are faced with ethical issues. Some other areas include removing life support from brain-dead patients and allowing elderly patients who do not want extraordinary treatment to die naturally. These issues often arise in hospitals. Hospitals deal with such problems by having the family's or patient's wishes reviewed by a special hospital committee. This committee includes medical members such as doctors, patient advocacy members such as social workers, and community members such as priests or rabbis. Together these people review each patient's case and decide whether the action requested by the patient or the patient's family is appropriate. A similar type of committee could be used on a national scale to make sure that stem cell research is conducted in an ethical way by reviewing individual projects. For example, as previously mentioned, the United Kingdom, Australia, and Canada have all established national committees to review, approve, and oversee stem cell research projects on an individual basis.

The major issues related to stem cell research are only going to become more prominent in the coming years, as advances in this area are made worldwide. We face two such issues now: Should we allow embryonic stem cell research, and if so, to what degree? Then, who should mind the shop and oversee and regulate the research process?

Timeline

1954   John Enders receives the Nobel Prize for demonstrating that the polio virus can be grown in embryonic kidney cells, signaling the beginning of embryonic cell research.

1956   Dr. E. Donnall Thomas of Cooperstown, New York, performs the first bone marrow transplant, treating leukemia in a patient with bone marrow from an identical twin.

1963   Ernest McCullough and James Till demonstrate that stem cells from mice can reproduce themselves.

1968   Dr. E. Donnall Thomas performs the first bone marrow transplant for a noncancerous disease, using a transplant between two siblings to treat severe combined immunodeficiency disorder (SCID), the lack of immune system cells.

1981   Two researchers isolate embryonic stem cells in mice: Gail Martin at the University of California–San Francisco and Martin Evans at the University of Cambridge.

1988   Edward A. Boyse and his team perform studies that demonstrate that umbilical cord blood can be used instead of bone marrow to regenerate immune system cells.

1995   F. H. Gage and colleagues at the Salk Institute for Biological Studies in La Jolla, California, demonstrate the ability of adult stem cells to differentiate into neurons in the brain.

1995 Passage of the Dickey Amendment makes it illegal to use federal money to pay for embryonic stem cell research.

1996 Ian Wilmut at the Roslin Institute in Scotland clones Dolly the sheep, the first mammal to be cloned.

1998 James Thomson and colleagues at the University of Wisconsin isolate stem cells in an embryo and subsequently develop a cell line.

1998 John Gearhart at Johns Hopkins University isolates embryonic germ (sex) cells from embryonic gonad (sex organ) tissue and develops a cell line.

2001 D. S. Kaufman and colleagues at the University of Wisconsin demonstrate that human embryonic stem cells can develop into blood cells.

2001 Advanced Cell Technologies, Inc., of Worcester, Massachusetts, produces the first cloned human embryos (grown only to the six-cell stage).

2001 President George W. Bush approves federal funding for stem cell research but restricts it to existing cell lines, banning funding for the development of new embryonic cell lines.

2003 D. A. Kerr and colleagues at Johns Hopkins University in Baltimore, Maryland, use human embryonic stem cells to restore muscle function in rats whose motor neurons were damaged by a virus.

2003 Dr. Songtao Shi of the National Institutes of Health isolates adult stem cells from children's primary teeth.

2005 New Jersey allocates $150 million in state funds to construct a stem cell research center; Connecticut allocates

$100 million over ten years for stem cell research; Illinois allocates $10 million to stem cell research.

2006 British scientists at University College, London, and London's Moorfields Eye Hospital successfully use stem cells implanted in the retina to improve the vision of blind mice.

2006 President George W. Bush vetoes a bill sent to him by Congress that would have expanded stem cell research eligible for federal funding to include research that uses discarded embryos.

Glossary

Alzheimer's disease A disease in which a person, usually elderly, loses intellectual functions and becomes increasingly confused, due to a buildup of abnormal tissue in the brain.

autologous Coming from oneself (from the Latin *auto*, which means "self"). Refers to material taken from the patient and returned to him or her during treatment.

black market An informal network of buyers and sellers who engage in illegal sales of a commodity.

cell line Successive generations of cells derived from one source and kept growing in a laboratory.

chromosomes Strands of genetic material made up of genes that carry the DNA code for specific traits.

clone A cell or organism with a genetic structure identical to that from which genetic material was taken.

debilitating Causing weakness or a loss of energy.

degenerative disease An illness in which tissue breaks down, causing an increasing loss of function over time.

diabetes A disease in which a person produces too little insulin, causing the sugar glucose to build up in the blood, damaging the body.

differentiate To develop specific characteristics.

efficacy Effectiveness.

embryo The earliest stage of a fertilized egg, before it develops any recognizable structure. In human beings, this occurs during the first two months.

embryonic stem cell A stem cell that comes from the tissue of an embryo.

implant To insert material from an external source into the body.

in vitro fertility (IVF) clinic A facility that combines eggs and sperm in a laboratory to create an embryo for implantation into a woman's womb so she can have a baby.

lupus A disease in which a person's immune system cells attack his or her body's organs and joints.

manslaughter Killing another person by accident or through negligence.

multiple sclerosis A disease in which the insulating layer of cells around nerve cells breaks down, leading to nerve, muscle, and sensory problems.

multipotent Able to change into more than one kind of cell.

Parkinson's disease A disorder in which the loss of brain cells that produce the chemical dopamine leads to muscle spasms, tremors, and trouble moving.

parthenote An early-stage embryo created by stimulating either an egg or sperm cell in a laboratory so that it will divide into a cluster of cells.

retina The layers of cells at the back of the eyeball that process visual information.

rheumatoid arthritis A disease in which a person's immune system cells attack his or her joints.

totipotent Able to change into all kinds of cells.

umbilical cord The tube that connects an embryo to its mother's blood supply in the womb.

unipotent Able to change into one kind of cell.

For More Information

American Association for the Advancement of Science
1200 New York Avenue NW
Washington, DC 20005
Web site: http://www.aaas.org

National Catholic Bioethics Center
6399 Drexel Road
Philadelphia, PA 19151
Web site: http://www.ncbcenter.org

National Center for Bioethical Literature
Kennedy Institute of Ethics
Georgetown University
Box 571212
Washington, DC 20057-1212
Web site: http://www.georgetown.edu/research/nrcbl

National Institutes of Health
9000 Rockville Pike
Bethesda, MD 20892
Web site: http://www.nih.gov
Stem cell information: http://stemcells.nih.gov/index.asp

Organization of Islamic Learning/International Association of
   Bioethics

Dr. Abdulaziz Sachedina
University of Virginia
Department of Religious Studies
Charlottesville, VA 22903
Web site: http://people.virginia.edu/~aas/home.htm

President's Council on Bioethics
1801 Pennsylvania Avenue NW, Suite 700
Washington, DC 20006
Web site: http://bioethics.gov

Stem Cell Research Foundation
22512 Gateway Center Drive
Clarksburg, MD 20871
Web site: http://www.stemcellresearchfoundation.org

WEB SITES

Due to the changing nature of Internet links, Rosen Publishing has developed an online list of Web sites related to the subject of this book. This site is updated regularly. Please use this link to access the list:

http://www.rosenlinks.com/ad/adsc

For Further Reading

Allman, Toney. *Great Medical Discoveries: Stem Cells*. San Diego, CA: Lucent Books, 2005.

Bellomo, Michael. *The Stem Cell Divide*. New York, NY: American Management Association, 2006.

Bevington, Linda K., Ray G. Bohlin, Gary P. Stewart, John F. Kilner, and C. Christopher Hook. *Basic Questions on Genetics, Stem Cell Research and Cloning: Are These Technologies Okay to Use?* Grand Rapids, MI: Kregel Publications, 2004.

Dowsdell, Paul. *Genetics: 21st Century Debates*. Chicago, IL: Raintree, 2001.

Jefferis, David. *Bio-Tech: Frontiers of Medicine*. New York, NY: Crabtree Publishing, 2001.

Jefferis, David. *Cloning: Frontiers of Genetic Engineering*. New York, NY: Crabtree Publishing, 1999.

Marzilli, Alan. *Stem Cell Research*. New York, NY: Chelsea House, 2007.

Panno, Joseph. *Stem Cell Research: Medical Applications and Ethical Controversy*. New York, NY: Checkmark Books, 2006.

Ruse, Michael, and Christopher A. Pynes, eds. *The Stem Cell Controversy: Debating the Issues*. Amherst, NY: Prometheus Books, 2003.

Tesar, Jenny. *Science on the Edge: Stem Cells*. Chicago, IL: Blackbirch Press, 2003.

Bibliography

Arnold, Wayne. "Singapore Acts as Haven for Stem Cell Research." *New York Times*, August 17, 2006. Retrieved December 14, 2006 (http://www.nytimes.com/2006/08/17/business/worldbusiness/17stem.html?ex=1313467200&en=a3268595bc581cd7&ei=5088&partner=rssnyt&emc=rss).

Bellomo, Michael. *The Stem Cell Divide*. New York, NY: American Management Association, 2006.

Bevington, Linda K., Ray G. Bohlin, Gary P. Stewart, John F. Kilner, and C. Christopher Hook. *Basic Questions on Genetics, Stem Cell Research and Cloning: Are These Technologies Okay to Use?* Grand Rapids, MI: Kregel Publications, 2004.

"EU to Fund Stem Cells." *International Herald Tribune*, July 24, 2006. Retrieved November 18, 2006 (http://www.iht.com/articles/2006/07/24/news/union.php).

Herold, Eve. *Stem Cell Wars*. New York, NY: Palgrave MacMillan, 2006.

Holland, Suzanne, Karen Lebacqz, and Laurie Zoloth, eds. *The Human Embryonic Stem Cell Debate: Science, Ethics, and Public Policy*. Cambridge, MA: MIT Press, 2001.

Jewish Law—Law and Policy. "Orthodox Union's Position re: Stem Cell Research." Retrieved November 27, 2006 (http://www.jlaw.com/LawPolicy/stemcellou.html).

Mayo Clinic. "Stem Cell Transplant." Retrieved November 12, 2006 (http://www.mayoclinic.com/health/stem-cell-transplant/CA00067).

Bibliography

National Institutes of Health. "Stem Cell Information." Retrieved November 12, 2006 (http://stemcells.nih.gov/info/faqs.asp).

Ruse, Michael, and Christopher A. Pynes, eds. *The Stem Cell Controversy: Debating the Issues*. Amherst, NY: Prometheus Books, 2003.

United States Conference of Catholic Bishops. "Stem Cell Research and Human Cloning: Questions and Answers." Retrieved November 18, 2006 (http://www.nccbuscc.org/prolife/issues/bioethic/stemcell/answers08052004.htm).

University of Michigan. "Stem Cells—Explained and Explored." Retrieved November 12, 2006 (http://www.lifesciences.umich.edu/research/featured/religious.html).

U.S. Food and Drug Administration. "Cellular Therapy: Potential Treatment for Heart Disease." Retrieved November 12, 2006 (http://www.fda.gov/cber/genetherapy/celltherapyheart.htm).

Index

A

abortion, 16, 18, 21, 26, 29, 44
Albert Lasker Award for Basic
   Medical Research, 11
Alzheimer's disease, 38
autoimmune disorders, 38

B

biophysicists, 11
black market, 29
blastocysts, 7, 10, 15–17, 26, 28
bone marrow, 5, 9, 11, 31–32, 39
"brain drain," 44

C

California Institute for
   Regenerative Medicine, 45
cell differentiation, 8, 9, 12, 33
chemotherapy, 32, 38
cloning
  autologous, 26, 28
  definition, 24
  and Dolly the sheep, 24
  mechanics of, 27
  opposition to, 28–30
  reproductive, 25–26
  therapeutic, 25–30, 49

D

debilitating, 42, 47

degenerative diseases, 30, 33, 37, 38
diabetes, 14, 38
discarded embryos, ethics of using,
   18–19, 22–23
dopamine, 35, 40

E

efficacy, 35
embryo, defining the status of,
   15–18

F

fertilization, 7

G

genetic defects/disorders, 34, 37, 38

H

Hodgkin's disease, 38

I

immune system, 9, 28, 33–35,
   38–39
immunosuppressive drugs, 35
Institute of Molecular and Cell
   Biology, 45
insulin, 14, 38
in vitro fertility (IVF), 10, 11, 15,
   18, 21, 26, 48–49
irradiation, 11

Index

ABOUT THE AUTHOR

Jeri Freedman has a B.A. from Harvard University and spent fifteen years working in companies in the biomedical and high-technology fields. She is the author of a number of other nonfiction books published by Rosen Publishing, as well as several plays and, under the name Foxxe, is the coauthor of two science-fiction novels. Freedman lives in Boston.

PHOTO CREDITS

Cover (left) © AFP/Getty Images; cover (right), pp. 7, 10, 19, 22, 25, 27, 30, 33, 37, 39, 45 © Getty Images; p. 9 © Gary D. Gaugler/Photo Researchers, Inc.; pp. 12, 15 © Rawlins/Custom Medical Stock Photo; p. 32 © Beebe/Custom Medical Stock Photo; pp. 43, 50 © AP Images.

Designer: Gene Mollica; **Editor:** Leigh Ann Cobb
Photo Researcher: Cindy Reiman